BRAINWASHING

Learn The Best Manipulation And Communication Techniques In Just 29 Days

Krystal Zhurov

Respective authors own all copyrights not held by the publisher.

The information herein is offered for informational purposes solely and is universal as so. The presentation of the information is without contract or any type of guarantee assurance.

The trademarks that are used are without any consent, and the publication of the trademark is without permission or backing by the trademark owner. All trademarks and brands within this book are for clarifying purposes only and are the owned by the owners themselves, not affiliated with this document.

Table of Contents

Introduction

Brainwashing is a colloquial term used with respect to the systematic attempts of Chinese Communists (and the Soviets, by implication) to convince non-believers to accept by coercive means communist allegiance, order and/or doctrine. More broadly, the term has been used for any tool designed to manipulate human thought or action against the individual's will, will or awareness. The term brainwashing derives from the Chinese expression Hai Nao (Hunter, 1951), which is most commonly used when referring to the Chinese Communist ideology reform (Szu Hsing Kao Tsao), a political indoctrination system focused on the premise that people who are not educated in a Communist society by definition have incorrect bourgeois views and attitudes, as well as muscular beliefs.

The word brainwashing started printing in an article published in September 1950 by the Miami News. The author Edward Hunter coined the word as a fairly down-market version of the Chinese hsi-nao, meaning purging the mind, and believed that China after the revolution was using unprecedented, subtle psychological techniques to drive the Chinese to the Communist Party.

He followed up with other articles and books and it seemed at least clear to the American public by the end of the Korean War that the US POWs that had collaborated with the enemy had no option. We were the innocent victims of an unprecedented exercise in mind control, a tactic first used to convince the Chinese to amend the Communist line and then to extend it to the prisoners of the enemy. The concept of "brainwashing" was released to a receptive audience. After all, it was a shock to see that so many of the American boys caught in Korea waved very broadly from the national line. The exact number of soldiers who went to some degree across the street differed according to the nervousness of various sources. Authors like the specialist in sychology, Josh Meerloo, who are afraid of mass manipulation, reported that 7190 US prisoners held in China have been influenced by

Communist propaganda, making confessions or signing petitions calling for a end to the war– although few Communists remained after the war and repatriation.

More dramatic versions of events mention a portion of the communist cause taken over by American POWs. The number was, however, high enough to convince Americans to support the reason for brainwashing and perhaps blind them to the just as clear fact that few British POWs, but very few Turks, who were treated in the same way, surrendered.

The repatriated US POWs, naturally, became a phenomenon that many psychiatrists and psychologists were able to study, keen to unravel what brainwashing was if anything, and if not, what had dramatically reduced their boys loyalty to the President and the country. It was the job of event researchers much later to say that the main brainwashing fear was spread by the CIA.

After all, Hunter, who coined the word, when he wrote on the topic was a CIA employee. He was not only a journalist, but a propaganda expert and a psychological warfare specialist at the Pentagon. He also used his biographical details to investigate, according to Scheflin and Option, writers of The Mind Manipur, in his first book, to send the message that the USA was targeted by an enemy using covert mental commands, and the message he provided. The subsequent actions of the CIA, when researching the ability of hypnosis, conditioning, drugs and so on to gain control of the mind, are not discussed in this book. The several books published on this topic seem to suggest that the CIA was humiliated and not illumined by its work.

Nevertheless, it is important to consider the roots of the term brainwashing because it is an interesting case in which a word is invented to encapsulate a concept (for whatever reason), and then instead of researching it, the word itself is the object of interest. Many psychological experts and courageous researchers examined the subject. Some focused on showing that brains could not be washed. Others conclude that brainwashing is a powerful, all-pervasive technique that first allows the person and then the environment to dominate.

Chapter 1

Concepts Of Brainwashing

What Is Brainwashing?

The term "brainwashing" was coined during the Korean War in the 1950s. It was used to illustrate how totalitarian regimes could indoctrinate US soldiers fully through a process of coercion and propaganda.

Brainwashing is the philosophy that the core beliefs, thoughts, affiliations and values of an individual can be substituted, to the extent that they have not control over themselves and can not think independently or critically.

Who's Actually Brainwashed?

In the book and movie The Manchurian Candidate Korean soldiers catch a successful senator during the war and wash their minds into a sleeping agent with the intention of killing the presidential aspirant.

The piece indicates that even an intelligent and powerful man can be brainwashed, but in reality, the other way around.

In general, it is people who are in some way vulnerable and therefore more likely to get swept up in a different way of thinking.

This could include:

- Lost your beloved by divorce or death.
- Being made redundant or fired from jobs.
- Be forced to live on the streets (particularly young people).
- They have a condition that they can't accept.

How Can You Be Brainwashed?

If you want to brainwash, you'll want to know more about you to exploit your values. You want to know what your strengths are, your weaknesses, who you trust, who is important to you and who you are listening to.

You begin the brainwashing process, which usually takes five steps:

1. Attack on Self-esteem
2. Isolation
3. Blind obedience
4. Us vs Them
5. testing

1. *Isolation:*

This is the first phase in brainwashing starts with loneliness, because it is unsafe to have friends and family around you. The last thing a brainwasher desires to do is to ask someone with a different opinion what you have to believe now. Isolation may begin by not permitting access to family or friends or by constantly checking where someone is and with whom they are.

2. *Self-esteem Attack:*

An individual who wants to brainwash a fellow person can do so only if the victim is vulnerable and has low self-confidence. A fractured person with the values of the brainwasher is much easier to rebuild. Therefore, the brainwasher must break down the self-esteem of the victim. Sleep deprivation, verbal or physical violence, misunderstanding or coercion may lead to this. A brainwasher can begin to monitor everything about the life of the victim, from food to sleep, to even using the bathroom.

3. *Us vs. Them:*

To break a person down and transform him in another image, we need to introduce an alternative way of life which is far more attractive than his present way. This is usually accomplished only by combining the victim with other brainwashed individuals, and thus endorsing the new regime. Or everybody could be wearing some sort of uniform, a set diet, or other rigid rules which promote group dynamics.

There are evidences to suggest that people are, by themselves, tribals and want to be part of a group, and that the brainwasher wants to convince her victim to lead the elite. A victim can also be given a new name, as in Patty Hearst, who was later kidnapped and renamed Tania by her captors who ultimately sided with her kidnappers when she was brainwashed.

4. Blind obedience:

The end objective of a brainwasher is blind obedience, where the individual has unquestioned orders. This is usually achieved by rewarding the person positively when they choose the brainwasher and punishing them negatively if they don't.

Singing a sentence over and over is also a good way to control a person. In addition to repeating the same sentence over and over, experiments have shown that analytics and repetitive parts of the brain are not synonymous. That means we can only do one thing or the other, so that we can avoid the questioning thoughts by chanting.

5. *Testing:*

A brainwasher should never believe his job is done because there are still situations where the victim will begin to recover self-sufficiency and start thinking again. Testing: The monitoring of their victims does not only show their brainwashing, it also helps brainwashers to see how much power their victims still have. Tests could include a criminal act such as the robbery of a shop or the burglary of a house.

Brainwashing is not only myth or the past, it is real and present in many aspects of society today. Yet, there are quite couple of things you can do to literally stop you from getting brainwashed, and this include the following:

- Don't believe anything you hear
- Don't believe in Hype
- Don't buy into paranoia or fear strategy
- Look for someone's agenda
- Check for subliminal messages
- Choose your own path

- Do your own analysis
- Hear your own instincts
- Don't choose the bandwagon
- Don't be afraid of being different

In case you believe that someone you know is brainwashed, remove them from their brainwasher, contact a specialist and help them.

Someone with brainwashing can recover from experience and historical study, which has shown that brainwashing is at best a temporary condition and does not leave a person's mind permanently damaged.

Chapter 2

How Brainwashing Work

American POWs are confirmed to have been brainwashed in prison camps by the Korean, Korean and Chinese captains. Several prisoners eventually admitted their allegiance to Communism by their own end of germ warfare, which they had not. At least 21 troops refused to return when they were returned to the United States. Total is impressive, but critics point out that in communist countries it has been 21 out of 20,000 prisoners. Will brainwashing work in a trustworthy way?

In psychology the study of the brainwashing, also referred to as the restructuring of the thinking, falls under "social influence". It is a set of ways in which people can alter the beliefs, opinions and actions of other people. For example, the enforcement approach aims to make a person's behavior change and doesn't affect him or her. It's the style of "Just do it". The education system (which is called the "propaganda process" when you don't believe what is being taught) is intended for the social influence of gold. It is designed to influence a shift in person's beliefs in the context of "do it because you know it is true" ("Do it because you know what it is right to do").

Since brainwashing is such an intrusive type of control, it requires complete isolation and reliance on the subject, so it is often said that brainwashing takes place in prison camps or totalitarian cultures. The agent (the brainwasher) must monitor the target (brainwasher) absolutely so that the agent's will depends on sleep patterns, feeding, bathing, and satisfying certain basic human needs. During the brainwashing process, the agent deliberately destroys the personality of the target so that it no longer works. The agent then replaces it with a new set of behaviours, attitudes and beliefs which function in the current environment of the target.

· Most psychologists think that brainwashing is possible in right circumstances, others think that brainwashing is impossible or at least less serious than that the media portrays. Many concepts of brainwash require the presence of threats of physical harm, and most radical societies do not practice true brainwashing under these definitions since recruits are generally not physically abused. Many meanings depend on "non-physical coercion and power" as a mechanism for affirming impact. Regardless of which description you use, a significant number of experts agree that even under ideal brainwashing conditions, the results of the procedure most often are short term the old identity of the brain-washing victim is not necessarily eradicated by the process but is concealed.

Some psychologists claim that the obvious conversion of the American POWs during the Korean War resulted from simplistic, unregulated coercion. And, indeed, most of the POWs in the Korean War were not converted into communism, leading to the question of trustfulness: is brainwashing a system that generates similar results across cultures and identities, or is primarily dependent on them? In the next segment, we'll study a brainwashing process overview by one expert and see what makes a target simple.

Chapter 3

Brainwashing Techniques

During the Korean War, journalist Edward Hunter coined the word "brainwashing" to describe the "re-education" methods used by the Chinese on American captured soldiers. Since then, this concept has been related to cults that often use a mixture of psychological techniques to comply with their leaders. Psychologist Margaret Singer argued that about 2,5 million people in the US alone are representatives of societies believed to use brainwashing methods at any time.

The notion of brainwashing was nevertheless still contentious. Hunter was involved with the intelligence community, and it was suggested that CIA promoted this term as an easy way of explaining why communism was growing rapidly at the time. The psychologists Robert Lifton and Edgar Schein concluded that US POWs who made anti-American comments were mainly against physical punishment and that POWs had not been especially effective in brainwashing. However, it is so imperative to be aware that some discussion is taking place on the exact nature and efficacy of brainwashing.

1. *Singing and Chanting*

The chanting Mantras are an important feature of many religions, especially Buddhism and Hinduism, and virtually every church has a kind of hymn-singing adoration. As each member of the congregation sings or speaks the same words, their voices merge into a chorus, creating a clear sense of unity and group identity. This, along with known singing effects like reduced heart rate and relaxation, could cast a positive light on the group worship experience.

However, in cult the repetitive repetition of short intonations is intended to twist, suppress logical thinking and trigger a state of trance. Enhanced suggestibility is a characteristic of such an atmosphere and failure to maintain trance is often accompanied by cultic penalties to ensure that ultra-conformist behaviour.

Linda Dubrow-Marshall and Steve Eichel psychologen have investigated how "the capacity of the converts to make decisions and assess new information is compromised if they respond to regular and long hypnotic inductions", adding that "continuous conferences, singing and singing are employed by most cults and serve to alter consciousness".

2. *Isolation*

Jim Jones moved to a remote municipality in Guyana in 1977 with around 1,000 members of the religious group of his People's Temple. About 400 kilometers of jungle have separated them from the American Embassy in Georgetown, the capital of Guyana. As Edward Cromarty points out, this isolation helped the cults "lose sight to the external values" and allowed Jones to incinerate a dystopian dictatorship of his own. Those who challenged Jones would be put in drug-induced comas, or even covered in pythons. In the night, rebellious children were lowered into baths.

Therefore, the physical isolation of the group was paralleled by a mental isolation. Far from the influence of their friends and family in the US, the people of the Temple have little choice but to secretly follow Jones toxic political agendas, even if they are interiorly dissatisfied with what's happening, with brutal punishment waiting for them if they fail to comply. The People's Temple Agricultural Project has full control over its members and enforced isolation, comparable to pariah states like North Korea or Albania prior to 1991.

3. *Dependency And Fear*

The abduction by Symbionese Liberation Army of Patty Hearst in 1974 is a classical example of brainwashing through addiction and fear. Hearst soon became a bank robber from a young radical and seemingly a dedicated terrorist organization leader. Hearst was locked up in a office after she was arrested, physically and sexually assaulted and repeatedly said that she could be murdered at any time. The SLA controlled her life completely. This dependency on its captors contribute to the famous effect of capture-bonding or Stockholm Syndrome. Months later, she became a religiously committed participant, even participating in the robbery of the bank in San Francisco.

After the police arrested Hearst, the prosecutor refused to admit that she was brainwashing and argued that the attackers were in full compliance. She was therefore sentenced to seven years imprisonment. Nevertheless, after two years President Carter commuted her sentence on the basis of her degrading experiences' as an inmate. While Hearst might be more impressive than most, her story shows how distressing experiences can transform the things we believe in and who we are.

4. *Activity Pedagogy*

How does a teacher promote their students good behavior and conformity? Often the solution consists of incorporating physical activity or sport into your teaching. Absorbed in jumping or running around, children are less likely to argue or trouble, and as a result tired. Aware of the trend, many societies sought to employ members as a means of control with endless series of tiring tasks. For instance, some alleged cultures such as Dahn Yoga are physical exercise systems on the surface. In Russia mass sports events such as stadium calisthenics were a distinctive feature of the soviet system and are related to a repressive state structure by historians.

What separates exercise pedagogy from pure sports is that a program or culture takes advantage of the improved mood and group identity felt during physical activity to incorporate concepts that could otherwise be met with skepticism. Exhaustion by exercise is yet another way of allowing peoples resistance to embrace dubious ideas.

5. *Fatigue and Slept Deprivation*

Our ability to make good decisions is crumbled by a mixture of sensory overload, disorientation and sleep deprivation. The multi-level marketing company Amway was accused of depriving its sleeping distributors during the weekend, with non-stop conferences going until early in the morning with only brief intermissions during which the bands play loud music with flashing lights.

A cultic strategy sometimes used in combination with sleep deprivation is to force participants to adopt special diets of low protein levels and other important nutrients. As a result, cults will always feel fatigued and unable to follow the demands of religious ideology. In the twentieth anniversary of the Aum Shinrikyo Sarin nerve gas attack, the Japan Times interviewed a former religious member who described the attempt to elected a religious leader to the Parliament "to eat one meal a day and sleep for some hours each night".

6. *Finger-pointing and Self-criticism*

During the Korean War, American soldiers, captured by the Chinese, had to engage in sessions of "criticism and autocracy" where they had to criticize their fellow prisoners, complain about their shortcomings and show insecurity about capitalism and the USA. The POWs thought the sessions were childish at first. But, over time they began to express real doubts about their patriotism and the legitimacy of the war.

Psychologist Robert Cialdini would describe the prisoners increasing anxiety as an effect of "the law of commitment" that says we try to maintain our behavior in line with our public statements because we don't want to be inconsistent or dishonest.

Although there were few victories, overall the brainwashing techniques of the Korean War were not particularly effective. At the end of the war, only 23 POWs rejected repatriation and the Chinese largely left the rehabilitation program a year prior to war. However, similar practices continued to be used domestically. The Tibetan Panchen Lama is shown above in one such public harassment session in 1964.

7. *Love Bombing*

Many cults want to intensify the sense that the world outside the party is unsafe and badly mistaken. In contrast, to be friendly they also use "love bombing" to make themselves look welcoming. Love bombing consists of showering new or future hires with lavish attention and affection. The word probably comes from either the Children of God or the Unifying Church, but it can now be extended to several different organizations. We feel strongly compelled to combat the kindness and generosity of others as a common occurrence in social psychology, so the feigned affection, encouragement and friendship shown in the forming cult to initiates are designed to create an increasing sense of duty, obligation and guilt.

Margaret Singer called it a major feature of cult, powerful as it is exactly what many modern cults are searching for their companion and validation. The psychologist Edgar Schein suggests that a cycle of« unfreezing and refrigeration » leads people to cults. In the non-freezing stage, a potential new cult member starts to abandon his old view of the world and is open to cult ideas. Upon refreezing, the society consolidates this new perspective. Schein points to the love of bombing as a crucial factor for refreezing: recruits who support religious ideology are rewarded with embracement and praise but are hindered if too many critical questions are asked.

8. *Mystical Manipulation*

The popular psychiatrist, Robert Jay Lifton claims that many cultures rely on "mystical coercion" to get full control over their followers. Mystical management includes manipulating events or knowledge by religious leaders to give the impression that they possess spiritual intelligence, divine favor, or magical powers. In other words, so-called religious leaders portray themselves as the unfailing messenger of God whose opinion should always be true and correct, and endorse it through impressive tricks and odd gimmicks.

George Roden, a leading Davidian leader in David's early challenges, exhumed a corps theatrically, which he promised to return to life, demonstrating his mighty powers. Then, he posed a challenge to his rival to do the same, but Koresh simply told the police instead of serious robbery. The police asked Koresh to collect evidence and a gunfight followed when the Koresh group tried to get into the compound where Roden held the body.

Koresh himself was known at the time as Vernon Howell, but later changed his name to indicate that he descended from the biblical King David. Rightly after Cyrus the Great, a Persian king who freed the Jews out of Babylonian captivity, he took the last name Koresh. Koresh created a messianic figure and persuaded his followers, if he had actually organized them, to attribute extraordinary events to divine intervention.

9. *Barratrous Violence*

Most societies employ attorneys to prosecute anyone who criticizes them publicly, no matter how trivial the criticism is. Of example, cult cases will typically be dismissed, because ex-cult leaders are often insolvent after they give their lives to the group. Therefore, many ex-cultists are unable to mount an effective legal counterattack.

In fact, mainstream journalists are wary of condemning religion or mentioning cults because of the persistent threat of legal proceedings. In 2003, Rick Ross received excerpts from the manuals of NXIVM, a self-improving organization charged with cults. Rick Ross put the excerpts online only to be hit with his garbage rifling by lawyers and investigators. Numerous NXIVM workers who left the organization faced heavy legal proceedings. A judge dismissed one of the lawsuits, finding out that NXIVM had simply tried, to leave, to be branded "suppressive", a word that refers to former members of the company, which NXIVM sees as its enemies and which has been subject to protracted litigation by the two major law firms and a phalanx of lawyers. L. In 1967, Ron Hubbard wrote that "we consider no opponents of Scientology without criminal record" and that prosecutions should be used to suppress these potentially culpable critics. HBO has, well aware of the consequences of the upheaval of Scientologists, hired 160 attorneys preemptively to protect their series Going Clear in 2015. Deterred from entering the courts, the church has launched a "brutal" campaign against the film-maker Alex Gibney.

10.   *Thought-Terminating Clichés*

The theory of totalitarian regimes frequently relies on "thought-terminating clichés" to enforce compliance with the subjects of a second major principle put forth by Robert Jay Lifton. The clichés "compress the farthest and most complicated of human problems into brief, highly reductive, definitive words." Lifton's classic example has been the "all-encompassing jargon" of communist regimes such as China and the Soviet Union, where language has become "abstract, highly structured, endless, and essentially" the language of thoughtlessness. Modern non-State organizations such as the Church of Scientology might have created phrases that are somewhat equivalent to Soviet jargon.

However, the most famous example of "thought-terminating clichés" is undoubtedly the Nazi officer Adolf Eichmann's court. The author Hannah Arendt commented in her renowned book on Eichmann and the' banality of evil' that the SS leader often spoke in phrases and clichés. Yet Arendt argued that the term was useless because he couldn't understand the nature of its crimes at all he would think of them only in the vocabulary of national Socialism. Arendt argued that "the German culture of eighty million citizens, by exactly the same means, same self-deception, deceit, and ignorance, was hidden from truth and factuality."

Chapter 4

The Element Of Manipulation

What is Manipulation?

The word "manipulation" would be seen by many as a negative or poor image. My point with the title 'Manipulation' is that you manipulate them regardless of the way you influence someone. If you force others to do something other than what they want to do, you personally exploit it.

The word manipulation has various meanings, some of which may be interpreted as negative. To exploit someone or something isn't bad in itself, it can only be bad if the intention is to hurt or create problems for someone.

The use of the word manipulation can be the following:

- ***Controlling*** our behavior, opinions and behaviors through self-sufficiency and self-hypnosis.
- To ***influence*** with a degree of pressure to get someone to think or do in our own way.
- To ***maneuver*** someone in a position of advantages where the outcomes are win / win for all involved parties and they are mutually acceptable. The idea of using your own power to influence someone is as old as our culture. Without going through all the story about hypnosis, trance induction, energy manipulation, etc. I will try to give you a very easy explanation about what hypnosis and trance is and how you can use it to your advantage.

Brainwashing and Manipulation

A detailed look at what took place at the Chinese prisoner of war camps in Korea is important to isolate the components of the so-called brainwashing mechanism. The US troops, who had been repatriated in 1953 and apparently worked with the enemy and, while shortly, were not the first to concentrate world attention on the trend of sudden political conversion. Between 1936 and 1938, Stalin show trials, where top bolchevic figures publicly admitted that they had not been able to commit spectacular crimes and even seemed to have freely accepted them as scum shocked much outside the country. It was unlikely that committed revolutionaries unexpectedly might have turned into groveling repentants. That some sinister mechanism was at work became a fact for Americans when their own people eventually replaced the Chinese, and in some instances, they admitted more fantastically that Americans had engaged in biological war against the Communists. The experts were therefore invited to try and find explanations.

Your detailed analysis of men's characteristics, their stresses and Chinese tactics provide the most comprehensive picture of the so-called brainwashing. In later years, claims that people like Patty Hearst or religious members were brainwashed have all been based on Korean findings.

Various analysts have highlighted the incidents and have sometimes drawn different conclusions. In August 1953 Edgar Schein, a MIT psychologist, obtained his personal data in Inchon, Korea, as repatriates were being processed, and on behalf of the USNS General Black, when the men had been on their way back to the USA for the first two weeks of September. In an article entitled' The Chinese prisoners of war indoctrination program: a study published in Psychiatry in 1956 on "brainwashing," he explained what had happened to the Korean soldiers, as they described it, and drew his own conclusions. As a result of his findings, he believed that Chinese brainwashing methods were nothing new and frightening. In reality they incorporated many conventional and well-known strategies in order to weaken opposition, such as group discussion, self-criticism, interrogation, remuneration and retribution, admissions, propaganda dissemination and information control. What was new was not the method, but the way to systematically combine a variety of tested methods.

The following summary of incidents in Korean POW camps is taken from the published version of Schein.

The Chinese attitude towards their prisoners varies from that of the North Koreans even at the beginning. While these were cruel to their prisoners, took off their uniforms, stripped them of daily and adequate food and punished or killed if a prisoner tried to resist them, the Chinese warmly welcomed the prisoners, and even congratulated them on being "liberated".

However, in the coming weeks and months, soldiers suffered severe physical and psychological strains and suggested in most of the Chinese's words or actions that these stresses would be avoided and life would be much more peaceful if they adopted a more 'cooperative' attitude towards their captors.

The men had to take long marches, which lasted maybe two weeks, on their way to the prison camp assigned to them. During the march they got little food and had to fight for what little food, clothes and shelters are on offer in order to survive, which, according to Schein, makes it impossible for them to sustain a group relationship. Throughout the process, the Chinese have lifted men's expectations by promising progress (though temporary prisons have not improved), and then shattered them by claiming that the UN is obstructive, or too many prisoners are uncooperative, and thus all have to suffer. Propaganda leaflets have been distributed and men have been compelled to sing communist songs.

When it finally reached the permanent camp, however, men were forced to suffer physical and psychological stress much more than they did so far.

(Schein here doesn't describe the tortures imposed on men, but Meerloo has mentioned a number which was included in the official American and British reports:

1. Standing by or sitting with legs stretching in utter silence from 4.30 to 11 p.m. and continuously being woken during the few hours required to sleep.

2. Ensure lonely containment in 5'x 3'x 2'x frames. One soldier was known to be in such a box for six months.

3. Having avoided drinks for days to help with self-reflection.

4. Be attached to a chain, the one end of which was placed over a beam and the other, the other around the ankles, like a hangman's noose. The inmate was then ordered to commit suicide if he stumbled or bent his knees.

5.   He had to kneel on jagged rocks, with his arms stretched above his head and holding a large stone.

6.   Be obliged, in one camp, to carry a thin piece of wood or metal in the mouth that a prisoner threw through the cell door through a window. Then the jailer will bang on the outside side of the wood or metal, possibly cracking his teeth or splitting his lip.

7.   Forced to march nude to the frozen river, where the water poured over their feet. Prisoners were then for hours to stand, frozen to the ground, dwelling on their crimes.

Chapter 5

How Do You Know If You Are Being Brainwashed, And What To Do.

In order to escape a life that is lived to an individual, and to achieve a success that is real, you must know how to avoid brainwashing Whether it is our political leanings or our perception of success, we are constantly being told about how we should think, live and work. It is easy, especially in moments of weakness, to unconsciously accept our own beliefs, live by them and blind ourselves to our own brainwashed tendencies.

You need to know how to avoid being brainwashed to escape a life lived for another and to experience real success.

Jim Rohn, a well-known American writer, businessman and inspiration speaker, said: "On average, there are five (5) people that you can literally spend the most time." If you agree with Rohn, you already understand where and how your belief system has been built. What you might not be somewhat be aware of is how much you unconsciously accept ideas that others make, rather than thinking about yourself through your belief system.

There are four ways to avoid brainwashing at work or in life:

1. *Know Yourself*

Most times, we don't take the time to know each other well. Take time to think about who you are, what your sphere of expertise is, what you care about and what you do not. Without this, it is easy to move in a direction which is not right for us. For example, you may have a parent that convinces you to be a doctor. But if you do not know what a good physician needs, and how your strengths correlate with this, you may blindly seek to be a physician, only to find out that this not the perfect job for you.

The better the message is delivered, the more likely you are to accept it. See if this environment is a true reflection of who you are, heart and soul when you join a group, employment or school.

2. *Have a Vision for Your Life and Your Career*

It's hard to be swayed by a dream when you are straightforward about it. If you have no dream, you are more likely to be affected by unique ideas or charismatic leaders in particular. Take the time to build your dream and make sure it is frequently visited again to make sure at every moment of your life it is right for you.

3. *Think and Be Worried*

We don't really think about our lives more often than not. We expect something to go wrong before we stop and remember that something needs to change. Instead of putting it off, start thinking about your life and career. Use your imagination to think about whether you can find a solution to a problem or take a new path for your life.

4. *Be Open, But Stay Grounded*

Being open means you know you don't know anything, and it's a great thing. Search for new information and remain rooted in how you digest it. Check, read, watch films or find information that excites you. Concentrate on the stuff that really concern you. When you feel particularly affected by someone, use it as a sign to dig deeper into it. Go beyond the surface by screening information.

Chapter 6

Recognizing Brainwashing And Avoiding It

Recognizing Brainwashing Skills

1. ***Note that those who try to brainwash others appear to prey on the vulnerable and the powerless.*** Not everyone is a candidate for mental control, but certain individuals are at different times more vulnerable to mental control. A professional manipulator knows what to look for and aims at people passing through a tough time in their lives or transforming themselves.

- People who have lost their jobs and worries for their future. Possible candidates include:

- Recently divorced individuals, particularly those who were bitter in divorce.

- Those with a lingering disease, especially those they do not understand.

- People who lost a loved one, particularly if they were very close to him and had few other friends.

- Young people first away from home. They are the favorites of the religious leaders.

- People who are perceived by their traditional peers as socially awkward. We sometimes seem to be alone, but we look like minded people who might be few and far away.

- A particular manipulative tactic is to find sufficient information about the person and his system of belief to justify the tragedy encountered in a way that is consistent with his belief system. This can be extended later to explain history generally through this belief system while subtly changing the understanding of the brainwasher.

2. ***Be aware that people are trying to isolate you from outside forces or***

someone you care about. When individuals with a personal tragedy or other major changes in life tend to feel depressed, a skillful brainwasher tends to intensify these feelings of loneliness. This isolation can take various forms.

- It may discourage young people in a cult from contacting their friends and family members.
- For another important person in an abusive relationship, it might mean that the victim will never be left out of sight or encourage contact with family and friends.
- In an enemy prison camp, inmates may be separated from each other when subject to subtle or transparent forms of torture.

3. ***Watch for self-esteem attacks on the victim.*** Brainwashing works only if the brainwasher is superior to the victim. This means that the victim must be broken down so that the brainwasher can recreate the

victim in its image. This can be achieved through intellectual, emotional or essentially physical means to wear the target physically and emotionally.

- Mental torture may start by lying to the victim and progress towards embarrassing or intimidating the victim. This type of torture can be done with words or actions from an expression of disagreement to a personal invasion of the victim.

- Emotional abuse is, of course, not kind but can begin with verbal insults and then proceed to badger, spit or dehumanize items like the removal of the photograph or simply look at the victim.

- Physical torture may involve famine, freezing, deprivation of sleep, beatings, maiming and so on. Physical torture is widely used in prisons in prison and "re-education" by abusive parents and partners.

4. ***Watch out for those who are trying to make "group members" more appealing than the outside world.*** In addition to the resistance of the victim, it is also important to offer an appealing alternative to what the victim knows before he comes into contact with the brainwasher. This can be done by various methods:

- Allowing only contact with other people who are already brainwashed. This generates a sort of peer pressure that causes the new victim to want to be like the new group and to be accepted. This can be enhanced by touch, rap, or group sex or by more stringent methods, for instance uniform dress code, controlled diet, or other strict rules.

- Repetition of the message by means of singing or repeating the same sentences over and over, often underlining some of the main words or phrases.

- Mimic the human pulse rhythm by the speech cadence or musical accompaniment of the thinker. This can be improved with not too dark or harsh lighting and a room temperature to induce relaxation.

- Never allow the victim to think. This can simply mean that the victim never has time to spend alone or harass the victim, thus avoiding questions, with repetitive lectures on things beyond comprehension.

- Present a mentality of "us versus them", where the thinker s right and the outside world is wrong. However, the main aim is to achieve blind obedience to which the victim must devote his wealth, life and goals to the brainwasher.

5. ***Recognize that brainwashers are often rewarded when they have "changed" the victim.*** When the victim is totally weakened and complacent, he or she may be retrained. Depending on the circumstances of brainwashing, it can take from several weeks to several years.

- The Stockholm syndrome is known as an extreme form of this complacency, where two bank robbers held four hostages in Sweden during 131 hours in 1973. After the hostages were released, they became so identified with the captors that one of the women collaborated with the captor and another formed a criminal legal defense fund. Patty Hearst, got kidnapped in 1974 by the Symbionese Liberation Army, is also a survivor of Stockholm syndrome.

6. ***Recognize new ways of thinking in the brain of the survivor.*** The retraining is largely done through some of the same methods of reward and punishment used by operators to break the victim down. Positive experiences are now being used to praise the victim for behaving like the brainwasher, while negative experiences are being used to punish the final traces of disobedience.

- One way of reward is to give a new name to the victim. This is usually connected to cult, but the SLA did so with Patty Hearst when he was named "Tania."

7. ***Rinse and Repeat***. However, brainwashing can be efficient and comprehensive, it is important for most brainwashers to test their control over their subjects. Based on the brainwasher's targets, power can be checked in various ways, resulting in deciding to what extent the reinforcement the victim needs to remain brainwashed.

- Extorting money is a way of checking and strengthening pockets in the brainwasher. Psychic medium Rose Marks used her influence over Jude Deveraux to make Deveraux cash and properties out of $17 million thus ruining the writer's career.

- Another criminal act is committed with or for the brainwasher. An example is Patty Hearst who accompanies the SLA on one of its robberies.

Identifying Someone That Has Brainwashed

1. ***Look for a combination of dependency and fanatism.*** The brainwash victims can seem to be focused on the group and its leader until they become obsessed. Also, without the help of the group or its leader, they appear incapable of solving problems.

Brainwashing victims unquestionably agree with whatever the community or leader decides, irrespective of the difficulty in or implications of lock-in. They may also withdraw from people who have no interest in brainwashing.

2. ***Look for signs of life withdrawal.***
Brainwashing victims are usually hesitant, unemployed, and devoid of any personality before they have been brainwashed. This is especially apparent in an abusive relationship both in established victims and in partners.

- Many victims can internalize their rage, resulting in depression and a host of fitness disorders, perhaps even suicide. Others may be upset at anyone they see as a cause of problems, often by verbal or physical conflict.

Washing Off Brainwashing

1. ***Make the subject aware of brainwashing.*** This awareness is often followed by denial and anxiety, because the subject starts to question things without practice. The subject should gradually become aware of how it has been manipulated.

2. ***Introduce the victim of brainwashing principles.*** Exposure to multiple options will give the subject a different, wider perspective, without overwhelming the subject with too many choices at a time, to question the convictions implanted by the brainwasher.

- Some of these contradictory ideas can come with their own manipulative forms in themselves. In such cases, it is useful to look as unbiased as possible forms of these ideas.

- Forcing the subject to relive the experience of brainwashing by having it done so, but giving the subject options to counteract brainwashing is a stronger form of this exposure. This type of therapy requires a psychodrama therapist.

1. ***Encourage the subject on the basis of new information to make his own decisions.*** At first, the subject might be afraid to decide itself or feel ashamed of taking the "bad" decision now or in the past. But in practice, this anxiety disappears.

Frequently Asked Questions And Answers On Brainwashing

1. Question: Is brainwashing a bad thing?

Answer: Yes. Community Answer Yes. If you control a person's mind to influence their emotions, it is harmful. You mess with your free will.

2. Question: Is there a way to reverse brainwashing effects?

Answer: Brainwashing victims frequently develop executive and cognitive disorders because their associated skills are less patterned to literally make them less likely to disobey or question orders. Victims have usually been conditioned not to respect or trust themselves, but to give the most faith and access to the abuser. The remedy is to comfort the victim and then replace the negative programming with counseling.

3. Question: Could I say when I was brainwashed?

Answer: Yes!! You have no more views, feelings, wishes, or actions contrary to the chief. You can then understand power of mind or brainwashing. There is a problem when the leaders wishes are paramount. You have the right to your own views and opinions. Once you are confronted by a position of "authority" you know that you no longer think for yourself.

4. Question: Why do people wash other people's brains?

Answer: Control and power over others. Community Answer. It is often to make up what they lack, which is positive self-esteem.

5. Question: My husband had been brainwashed and done after a work accident. He then began a new career in which he was brainwashed in two months in an extreme religion and a flat earth world. What can I do?

Answer: First, try to get him to remember the good times he was monitored before any of these incidents. Let him know that these days you miss and then the guy he was. You should remind him of how important it was for him to take responsibility and appreciate the decisions he took at the time. However, concerning this I would suggest that in case you now want to take a joint decision, you believe you have to contact your religious leader, and you want him to decide for himself.

6. *Question:* What can I do in case I accept the brainwashing of my husband? It's impossible now to get rid of it.

Answer: Discuss the specifics of your situation with someone. An external source will give you some clarification. Ideally, this person should be a mental health consultant.

7. *Question:* What can I do if I think my wife washes my brain and it becomes more difficult to break the abuse?

Answer: You will believe in yourself. Learn to be comfortable and ask what you want.

8. *Question:* Can a graphic brainwash movie brutalize people?

Answer: No. This can somewhat takes days, weeks, months, or even years for brainwashing. A 2-hour film won't do anything. Nevertheless, you can become more violent by desensitizing yourself to aggression.

9. *Question:* How can I say if my pastor is brainwashing?

Answer: Recognize that the power that is under you and your priest is the word of God, the Bible. Know the Bible and its fundamental principles and teachings. However, pay attention when reading it to what it means (not just what your preacher said to you); understand the immediate meaning and the context of the whole of the Bible.

10. *Question:* In two weeks our son gets married, and we have the feeling he's brainwashed. What can we do?

Answer: You can have a rational and honest conversation with him, but eventually you are an adult and must be allowed to take decisions your own, even if you disagree with them. Group Response

Tips

• The results of brainwashing can be reversed without the help of someone else. Studies by psychiatrist Robert J. Lifton and psychologist Edgar Schein in 1961 found that few of these soldiers who had been subjected to Chinese brainwashing techniques had actually gone to the communism, and of the few who had gone away from those views.

Warnings

• Hypnosis is not associated with brainwash though forms of hypnosis can be used in brainwashing. Brainwashing uses a shallow scheme of remuneration and punishment for its perpetrators and seeks to continuously tear down the resistance of the victims.

Hypnosis usually begins to calm, requires a relaxation of the mind, and does not usually involve incentives and punishments. Given its scope, hypnosis often works faster than brainwashing on a subject.

- Many professionals known as de-programmers were often hired by parents in the 1980s to physically save their children from worship. Although several of these de-programmers used brainwashing-style methods to counter-indoctrinate the "rescued" subjects.

- A de-programming technique, however, have often been unsuccessful as brainwashing needs to be gradually improved and they have been accused of criminal charges by a target.

Chapter 7

Brainwashing In Abusive Relationships

Sometimes torture feels like being in an unhealthy relationship. Sometimes it's because the actions of your partner sounds like torture devices used instead by lethal enemies.

The psychological dictionary defines brainwashing as "manipulating and altering one's thoughts, attitudes and beliefs." It decreases one's ability to defend oneself psychologically and makes it easier for another to manipulate it.

Brainwashing is an example of how coercion resembles violence in ties. Brainwashing makes controlling a target person easier. And the person finds it harder to free himself from the relationship. Abusive people are often able to throw their targets into a trance that makes it hard for them to think clearly. Targets of violence will start taking on and losing the views of the victim.

A man or woman who has little or no time to recover and is busy responding to the demands may not have a lot of mental energy left over. Both may be overwhelmed with the partner's version of events to the point that their viewpoints are difficult to hold. The discomfort that can be triggered by violence makes it difficult to think clearly.

Albert Biderman, in 1956, researched how prisoner of war camp staff received tactical information from U.S. prisoners of the Korean War, work with propaganda, and comply with false confessions. Biderman noted that it is not appropriate to "induce conformity" to inflict physical pain, but to this end psychological manipulation was extremely effective. Within his study, he described what became known as the "Biderman's Chart of Coercion." Many Biderman's chart identified the aspects of brainwashing which lead to different situations, including partner abuse. The strategies found in his map may be correlated with other forms of abuse of partners.

In the map of the Coercion system, Biderman summarized the brainwashing mechanisms:

- Monopolization of perception (fixes attention to immediate predicament; eliminates stimuli)
- Induced debilitation or fatigue
- Isolation
- Occasional Indulgences (Provides encouragement to comply, inhibits adjustment to deprivation)
- Threats
- Degradation
- Enforcing trivial demands
- Exercising superiority

Each element can be able to distort reality, interfere with perception, reduce the self-confidence of a person and achieve compliance.

The prisoner and the prisoner are rivals in a prisoner of war camp. Servants and women are usually trained in brainwashing if they are captured by the enemy forces.

The partners should be on the same side in a romantic relationship. It is reasonable to expect and give your partner respect, understanding and compassion. The relationship inevitably leads to a susceptibility to a manipulative or self-centered partner's emotional brainwashing. It's unpredictable. It can hang on you.

Chapter 8

Narcissistic Brainwashing

A narcissistic relationship entails vicious emotional abuse. Through brainwashing their victims, narcissists are able to do that. They use a variety of methods to monitor their significant others. We "heart" their prey first, then intimidate, undermine, blame move, criticize, exploit, verbally attack, dominate, chase, flee, withhold their love and affection, and gas their victims.

Sam Vaknin, a self-professed narcissist and author of "Malignant Self-Love, Narcissism Revisited", explains what the narcissist is doing to manipulate his victim:

"He infiltrates his defense, shatters his self-esteem, confuses and confuses her, demeans and degrades her. It is occupying their territory, abuses their trust, exhausts their wealth, damages their loved ones, threatens their stability and safety, puts them in fearful states of mind, frightens them by their intelligence, refuses love and sex from them, prevents fulfillment and frustrations; humiliates, insults them both privately and in public. Very often, the narcissist behaves with sadism as an illuminated motive in his victim's wellbeing. He plays the doctor (he made up totally) in her psychopathology. He is the Guru, the avuncular or father figure, the teacher, the only true friend, the old and the experienced. All this in order to weaken its defenses and bring its disintegrating nerves under attack. The narcissistic form of sadism is so subtle and toxic that it could well be called the most harmful.

-    ***Love bombing***

This is an attempt to influence an individual with prodigious displays of attention and affection. It was used to refer to offenders in romantic relationships who showered their victims in the early stages of their relationship with attention, gifts and affection. One of the victims explains this as follows: The narcissist partner thought the world of myself, came to me to help me and was trying to do anything for me. They can't keep the façade long. But if you don't know better, they are masters to get you hooked. "The feeling of" love that you have is more powerful than usual because the narcissist first fills you with love and then maintains and then gives you something, which over time changes you- it's a kind of manipulation, manipulating, and brainwashing. There's no chance you enjoyed it. But you can't love the narcissists back. What happens in these kinds of relationships is that you feel so trapped that you don't hear the warnings in your mind.

- ***Degradation***

Narcissists degrade their victims and dismiss their self-esteem that can make it difficult to resist their control strategies. Tactics like sarcasm, criticism, calling names, referral, degradation, undue blame, screaming, threats and humiliation are used. With time, the continuing verbal and emotional assaults undermine the victims, eroding their sense of self-confidence and self-esteem, making the narcissists more dominant and therefore more regulated.

-   *Verbal Assaults*

Which involves therapy, abuse, criticism, shouting, yelling, intimidation, unfounded blame, and sarcasm and humiliation. It also exaggerates your flaws and makes you famous. This type of abuse erodes your self-confidence and self-worth over time.

The abuser uses the terror, remorse, sympathy, beliefs, or other "hot buttons" to get what they want. Emotional blackmail These may include threats to terminate the relation, the "cold shoulder" or other methods of fear.

-   *Dominance demonstration*

A narcissist believes and plans a position of being omnipotent and omnipotent, which can persuade the victim to resist the narcissist. You must be in charge of others, you will do all you can and will use threats or other means to apply them. Ultimately, the victim loses her respect for herself.

- *Threats If victims are incompatible*

Narcissists will cause their victims to feel anxious and despaired by threats and intimidation. This encourages the victim to respond to the narcissist's unreasonable demands or intimidation.

The abuser puts unreasonable demands on you and expects you to set all else aside (including your children) in order to satisfy its "very significant" needs. It could be a prerequisite for constant attention, frequent sex or spending all your free time with the person. However, this is never enough, no matter how much you offer. You are constantly criticized and blamed for not meeting all the needs of this individual.

- *Isolation*

This takes away all social support that increases the victim's resilience. The narcissist holds the victim unaware of what is occurring (for example, by taking full control of the finances of the family, by creating plans which the victim can not realize, by telling others lies about them, etc.). The narcissist insists on manipulating the time and physical environment of his partner in order to try to curb his natural behavior and feelings. You may demand that your partner gives up those interests, social activities or jobs. They can even insist on their partner moving away to a new location that isolates the victim further from their friends or family.

- ***Total control of expectations***

Abusers may convince victims that elements of the victim's character and/or behavior, which focuses on what the narcissist does, are' false.' The narcissist will then monitor the type of information and stimuli that the victim has access to by using the isolation of the victim.

- ***Unpredictable responses***

Drastic changes in mood or unexpected emotional outbursts are used to confuse and alarm the victim. This conduct gives the victim the impression that he is always on the edge. You just wait for the other shoe to fall and can never know what is expected. We remain extremely alert, waiting for the next anger or mood of the other person. Living this way is extremely demanding, causing anxiety and the abused person is constantly afraid, unsettled and unbalanced.

- *Constant Confusion*

A narcissist may intentionally dispute and fight with others. Often they are addicted to "drama", because it excites.

- *Gas Lightning*

The narcissist may deny that certain events have occurred, or certain statements have been said. The victim knows otherwise, but the other party ignores his beliefs, memory, and wellbeing. That makes them think they're crazy or lose sight of themselves.

- *Implementing trivial demands*

They can make a great deal of confusion over trivial matters in order to put the victim in the habit of compliance.

- *Occasional indulgences*

The narcissist may give 'treats' or show kindness to promote and facilitate compliance.

In the end, the victim gets brainwashed because she assumes that her partner is somehow supremely intelligent and strong. The fact is that the narcissist is a dysfunctional, malicious and violent person. Narcissists and other criminals are using these strategies since they are highly effective in achieving their control goals and coercion.

Conclusion

Conclusively, it is easy to stay lazy and do the job to keep others brainwashing. This is somewhat part of being human, we always want to be involved and the more will agree with whatever with people around us the more likely we experience brainwashing. The key is to know it before or as it happens. Please spend time talking to yourself. If you do that, it will be much harder for anyone to persuade you that you're not anyone.